MW01110339

The little book of

IRISH SONGS

THE TUNEBOOK SERIES

Arrangements © 2016 Stephen Ducke

All Rights Reserved

www.tradschool.com

CONTENTS

INTRODUCTION

Welcome to this, the second volume in the Tunebook Series, a series of quality and affordable Irish- and Celtic-themed music books. The songs in this volume are among the most popular traditional folk songs and ballads from Ireland, as heard in pub sessions and played by groups the world over. They are presented in simple and easy-to-read format, arranged for guitar and voice, with individual or group practice specifically in mind. An indication of tempo is given for each tune - this is to be seen as just that, an indication or a general rule, and not an absolute direction! In practice, many Irish tunes can be played faster or slower - this will depend on the musicians' individual musical styles and tastes. A basic guitar chord sheet is given on page 4 - this too is to be seen as a starting-point, as different voicings and chord-shapes can also be used.

The songs in this volume represent the most popular pub songs, ballads and drinking songs from Ireland, with classic titles such as Whiskey in the Jar, The Wild Rover, The Bold Fenian Men or the Galway races. Whether you're a student, a teacher or a professional musician, you are encouraged to delve into the melodies in this collection, adapt them, make them your own, in the way that is unique to Irish and Celtic music. This collection represents the seed, that you will nurture to blossom in the way done by countless musicians, be they from Ireland or elsewhere, for the past two hundred years.

GUITAR CHORDS USED IN THIS SERIES

G

D

C

A

E

Em

Am

Bm

Bm

D7

A7

Am7

F

Dm

The Cliffs Of Dooneen

You may travel far far from your own native home
Far away across the mountains far away o'er the foam
But of all the fine places that I've ever seen,
There's none to compare with the Cliffs of Dooneen

Take a view oer the water fine sights you'll see there
You'll see the high rocky slopes on the West coast of Clare
The towns of Kilrush and Kilkee can be seen
From the high rocky slopes at the Cliffs of Dooneen

Its a nice place to be on a fine Summer's day
Watching all the wild flowers that ne'er do decay
The hare and lofty pheasant are plain to be seen
Making homes for their young 'round the Cliffs of Dooneen

Fare thee well to Dooneen fare thee well for a while
And to all the fine people I'm leaving behind
To the streams and the meadows where late I have been
And the high rocky slopes of the Cliffs of Dooneen

Arrangements © 2016 www.tradschool.com

Whiskey in the Jar

As I was go-ing o-ver the far famed Ker-ry moun-tains, I

met with Cap-tain Far-rell and his mo-ney he was coun-ting, I

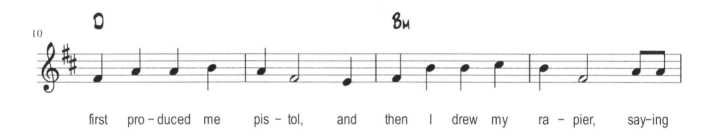

first pro-duced me pis-tol, and then I drew my ra-pier, say-ing

'Stand and de-li-ver for you are a bold de-cei-ver!' With me

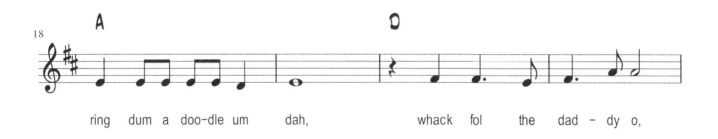

ring dum a doo-dle um dah, whack fol the dad-dy o,

Arrangements © 2016 www.tradschool.com

whack   fol   the   dad - dy   o,   there's   whis - key   in   the   jar!

As I was a going over the far famed Kerry mountains
I met with captain Farrell and his money he was counting
I first produced my pistol and I then produced my rapier
Saying "Stand and deliver for you are a bold deceiver"

Chorus:
With me ring dum a doo-dle um dah,
Whack fol the dad-dy o,
Whack fol the dad-dy o,
There's whiskey in the jar

I counted out his money and it made a pretty penny
I put it in me pocket and I took it home to Jenny
She sighed and she swore that she never would deceive me
But the devil take the women for they never can be easy (Chorus)

I went up to my chamber, all for to take a slumber
I dreamt of gold and jewels and for sure 't was no wonder
But Jenny drew me charges and she filled them up with water
Then sent for captain Farrell to be ready for the slaughter (Chorus)

'Twas early in the morning, just before I rose to travel
Up comes a band of footmen and likewise captain Farrell
I first produced me pistol for she stole away me rapier
I couldn't shoot the water, so a prisoner I was taken (Chorus)

Now there's some take delight in the carriages a rolling
and others take delight in the hurling and the bowling
but I take delight in the juice of the barley
and courting pretty fair maids in the morning bright and early (Chorus)

If anyone can aid me 'tis my brother in the army
If I can find his station in Cork or in Killarney
And if he'll go with me, we'll go rovin' through Killkenny
And I'm sure he'll treat me better than my own a-sporting Jenny (Chorus)

Arrangements © 2016 www.tradschool.com

Boolavogue

rock   with   a   war   ning   cry: Arm!   Arm!"   he

cried,   "For   I`ve   come   to   lead   you   –   for

Ire   –   land`s    free    –    dom    we`ll   fight   or   die!"

At Boolavogue as the sun was setting,
O`er the bright may meadows of Shelmalier,
A rebel hand set the heather blazing,
and brought the neighbours from far and near;

Then Father Murphy from old Kilcormack
Spurred up the rock with a warning cry:
"Arm! Arm!" he cried, "For I`ve come to lead you,
for Ireland`s freedom we`ll fight or die!"

He lead us on against the coming soldiers,
And the cowardly Yeomen we put to flight,
`Twas at the Harrow the boys of Wexford
Showed Bookey`s regiment how men could fight;

Look out for hirelings, King George of England,
Search every kingdom where breathes a slave,
For Father Murphy of County Wexford,
Sweeps o`er the land like a mighty wave.

We took Camolin and Enniscorthy,
And Wexford storming drove out our foes,
`Twas at Slieve Coilte our pikes were reeking
With the crimson blood of the beaten Yeos.

At Tubberneering and Ballyellis,
Full many a Hessian lay in his gore,
Ah! Father Murphy had aid come over,
The Green Flag floated from shore to shore!

At Vinegar Hill, O`er the pleasant Slaney,
Our heroes vainly stood back to back,
and the Yeos at Tullow took Father Murphy,
and burnt his body upon a rack.

God grant you glory, brave Father Murphy,
And open Heaven to all your men,
the cause that called you may call tomorrow,
in another fight for the Green again.

The Wild Rover

I've been a wild ro-ver for ma-ny's the year And I

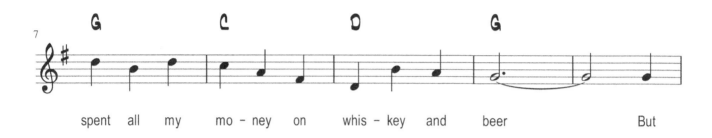

spent all my mo-ney on whis-key and beer But

now I'm re-tur-ning with gold in great store And I

ne-ver will play the wild ro-ver no more And it's

no, nay, ne-ver No nay ne-ver no

more   Will I play   the wild rov – er   No

ne – ver   No more.

I've been a wild rover for many's the year
And I spent all my money on whiskey and beer
But now I'm returning with gold in great store
And I never will play the wild rover no more

Chorus:
And it's no, nay, never,
No, nay never no more
Will I play the wild rover,
No never no more

I went in to an alehouse I used to frequent
And I told the landlady my money was spent
I asked her for credit, she answered me nay
Such a customer as you I can have any day

(Chorus)

I took up from my pocket, ten sovereigns bright
And the landlady's eyes opened wide with delight
She says "I have whiskeys and wines of the best
And the words that you told me were only in jest"

(Chorus)

I'll go home to my parents, confess what I've done
And I'll ask them to pardon their prodigal son
And, when they've caressed me as oft times before
I never will play the wild rover no more

(Chorus)

Follow Me Up To Carlow

Up with hal - berd, out with sword On we go for, by the Lord

Fiach Mc-Hugh has giv - en the word "Fo-llow me up to Car - low"

Lift Mac Cahir Og your face,
You're broodin' o'er the old disgrace
That Black Fitzwilliam stormed your place
and drove you to the ferns
Gray said victory was sure,
And soon the firebrand he'd secure
Until he met at Glenmalure
with Fiach McHugh O'Byrne

Chorus:
Curse and swear, Lord Kildare,
Fiach will do what Fiach will dare
Now Fitzwilliam have a care,
Fallen is your star low
Up with halbert, out with sword,
on we go for, by the Lord
Fiach McHugh has given the word
"Follow me up to Carlow"

See the swords of Glen Imaal,
They're flashing o'er the English Pale
See all the children of the Gael,
Beneath O'Byrne's banner
Rooster of a fighting stock,
Would you let a Saxon cock
Crow out upon an Irish Rock,
Fly up and teach him manners

(Chorus)

From Tassagart to Clonmore,
There flows a stream of Saxon gore
And great is Rory Og O'More
At sending loons to Hades
White is sick, Gray is fled,
And now for black Fitzwilliam's head
We'll send it over, dripping red
to Liza and her ladies

(Chorus)

Bold Fenian Men

♩ = 70

'Twas down by the glen-side, I – met an old wo-man She was

pick-ing young ne-ttles and she scarce saw me com-ing I

list-ened a while to the song she was humm-ing Glo-ry

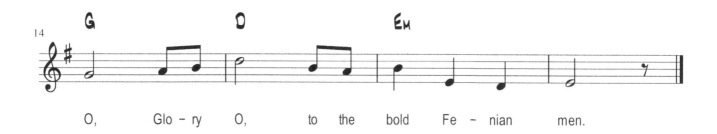

O, Glo-ry O, to the bold Fe-nian men.

Arrangements © 2016 www.tradschool.com

'Twas down by the glenside, I met an old woman
She was picking young nettles and she scarce saw me coming
I listened a while to the song she was humming
Glory O, Glory O, to the bold Fenian men

'Tis fifty long years since I saw the moon beaming
On strong manly forms and their eyes with hope gleaming
I see them again, sure, in all my daydreaming
Glory O, Glory O, to the bold Fenian men.

When I was a young girl, their marching and drilling
Awoke in the glenside sounds awesome and thrilling
They loved poor old Ireland and to die they were willing
Glory O, Glory O, to the bold Fenian men.

Some died on the glenside, some died near a stranger
And wise men have told us that their cause was a failure
They fought for old Ireland and they never feared danger
Glory O, Glory O, to the bold Fenian men

I passed on my way, God be praised that I met her
Be life long or short, sure I'll never forget her
We may have brave men, but we'll never have better
Glory O, Glory O, to the bold Fenian men

Arrangements © 2016 www.tradschool.com

Arthur McBride

Arrangements © 2016 www.tradschool.com

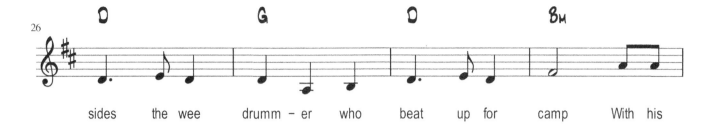

sides   the wee   drumm – er   who   beat   up for   camp   With his

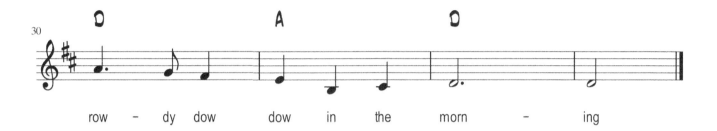

row – dy dow   dow   in   the   morn   –   ing

I had a first cousin called Arthur McBride
He and I took a stroll down by the by the sea side
A seeking good fortune and what might be tide
'Twas just as the day was a dawning
After resting we both took a tramp
We met Sergeant Harper and Corporal Cramp
Besides the wee drummer who beat up for camp
With his rowdy dow dow in the morning

Says he me young fellows if you will enlist
A guinea you quickly have in your fist
Likewise the crown for to kick the dust
And drink the king's health in the morning
From a soldier he leads a very fine life
He always is blessed with a charming young wife
And he pays all his debts without sorrow or strife
And always lives happy and charming

Ah now me bold sergeant we are not for sale
We'll make no such bargain, your bribe won't avail
We're not tried of our country we don't care to sail
Although that your offer is charming
And if we were such fools as to take the advance
This right bloody slander would be our poor chance
For the Queen wouldn't scruple to send us to France
Where we would be shot with out warning

He says me young fellows if I hear but one word
I instantly now will out with my sword
And into your body as strength will afford
So now my gay devils take warning
But Arthur and I we took in the odds
We gave them no chance
For to launch out their swords
Our whacking shillelaghs came over their heads
And paid them right smart in the morning

As for the wee drummer we rifled his pouch
And we made a football of his rowdy dow dow
And into the ocean to rock and to roll
And bade it a tedious returning
As for the old rapier that hung by his side
We flung it as far as we could in tide
To devil I pitch you said Arthur McBride
To temper your steel in the morning

Arrangements © 2016 www.tradschool.com

Botany Bay

Fare - well to your bricks and mor - tar, fare - well to your dir - ty lies Fare

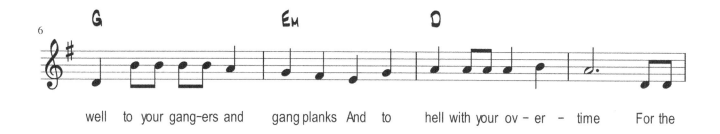

well to your gang-ers and gang planks And to hell with your ov - er - time For the

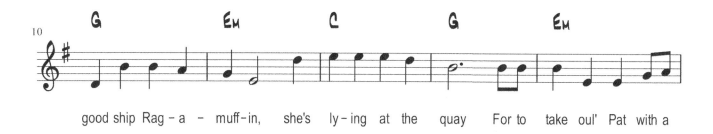

good ship Rag - a - muff-in, she's ly - ing at the quay For to take oul' Pat with a

shov - el on his back To the shores of Bota - ny Bay

Arrangements © 2016 www.tradschool.com

Chorus:
Farewell to your bricks and mortar, farewell to your dirty lies
Farewell to your gangers and gang planks
And to hell with your overtime
For the good ship Ragamuffin, she's lying at the quay
For to take oul Pat with a shovel on his back
To the shores of Botany Bay

I'm on my way down to the quay, where the ship at anchor lays
To command a gang of navies, that they told me to engage
I thought I'd drop in for a drink before I went away
For to take a trip on an emigrant ship
To the shores of Botany Bay

(Chorus)

The boss came up this morning, he says "Well, Pat you know
If you don't get your navies out, I'm afraid you'll have to go"
So I asked him for my wages and demanded all my pay
For I told him straight, I'm going to emigrate
To the shores of Botany Bay

(Chorus)

And when I reach Australia I'll go and look for gold
There's plenty there for the digging of, or so I have been told
Or else I'll go back to my trade and a hundred bricks I'll lay
Because I live for an eight hour shift
On the shores of Botany Bay,

The Galway Races

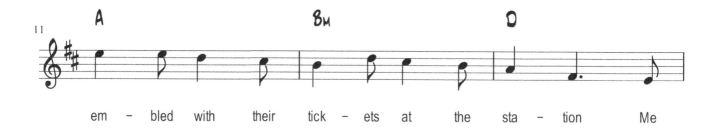

Arrangements © 2016 www.tradschool.com

ra - ces With me wack fol the do fol the

di - ddl - y id - le day

As I went down to Galway Town
To seek for recreation
On the seventeenth of August
Me mind being elevated
There were passengers assembled
With their tickets at the station
And me eyes began to dazzle
And they off to see the races

Chorus:
With me wack fol the do fol
The diddle idle day

There were passengers from Limerick
And passengers from Nenagh
The boys of Connemara
And the Clare unmarried maiden
There were people from Cork City
Who were loyal, true and faithful
Who brought home the Fenian prisoners
From dying in foreign nations (Chorus)

And it's there you'll see the pipers
And the fiddlers competing
And the sporting wheel of fortune
And the four and twenty quarters
And there's others without scruple
Pelting wattles at poor Maggie
And her father well contented
And he gazing at his daughter (Chorus)

And it's there you'll see the jockeys
And they mounted on so stably
The pink, the blue, the orange, and green
The colors of our nation
The time it came for starting
All the horses seemed impatient
Their feet they hardly touched the ground
The speed was so amazing! (Chorus)

There was half a million people there
Of all denominations
The Catholic, the Protestant, the Jew,
the Presbyterian
Yet there was no animosity
No matter what persuasion
But failte hospitality
Inducing fresh acquaintance (Chorus)

Bucket of the Mountain Dew

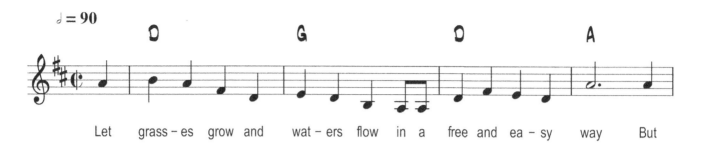

Let grass – es grow and wat – ers flow in a free and ea – sy way   But

give me e-nough of the rare old stuff that's brewed near Gal – way Bay   Come

police – men all from Don – e – gal, from Sli – go and Lei – trim too   We'll

give them the slip and we'll take a sip Of the rare old Moun – tain Dew   Hi di

didd-ly – id – le-um, didd-ly – doo-dle-id – le-um, didd-ly – doo – ri – didd-lum – deh   Hi di

Arrangements © 2016 www.tradschool.com

didd—ly – id – le–um,   didd–ly – doo–dle–id – le –um,   didd–ly – doo – ri – didd–l –um – deh

Let grasses and waters flow in a free and easy way,
But give me enough of the rare old stuff that's brewed near Galway Bay,
Come policemen all from Donegal, Sligo and Leitrim too,
We'll give them the slip and we'll take a sip
Of the rare old Mountain Dew

Chorus:
Hi di-diddly-idle-um, diddly-doodle-idle-um, diddly-doo-ri-diddlum-deh
Hi di-diddly-idle-um, diddly-doodle-idle-um, diddly-doo-ri-diddlum-deh

At the foot of the hill there's a neat little still,
Where the smoke curls up to the sky,
By the smoke and the smell you can plainly tell
That there's poitin brewin' nearby.
For it fills the air with a perfume rare,
And betwixt both me and you,
As home we stroll, we can take a bowl,
Or a bucket of the Mountain Dew

(Chorus)

Now learned men who use the pen,
Have sung the praises high
Of the rare poitin from Ireland green,
Distilled from wheat and rye.
Put away with your pills, it'll cure all ills,
Be ye Pagan, Christian or Jew,
So take off your coat and grease your throat
With a bucket of the Mountain Dew.

(Chorus)

Arrangements © 2016 www.tradschool.com

The Lark in the Morning

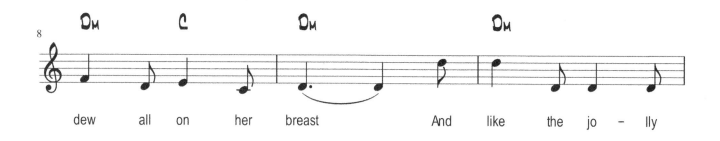

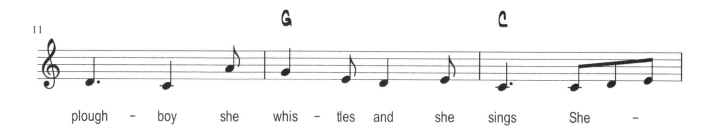

Oh, the lark in the morning she rises off her nest,
She goes off in the air with the dew all on her breast;
And like the jolly ploughboy she whistles and she sings,
She goes home in the evening with the dew all on her wings.

Oh, Roger the ploughboy he is a dashing blade,
He goes whistling and singing all through the leafy glade;
He nests at dark at Susan's, she's handsome, I declare,
She's far more enticing than the birds all in the air.

As they were riding home from the fair all in the town,
Well, the madder was so kissable and the heather was mowed down;
Twas there they jumped and tumbled all in the new mown hay,
Said, "Take me now or never," this young lass she did say.

When twenty long weeks had all of them gone past,
Well, her mother asked the reason why she thickened 'round the waist;
"It was the jolly ploughboy," this young lass she did say,
"He caused me for to tumble all in the new-mown hay."

So, here's a health to the ploughboy wherever you may be,
Would you like to have a bonnie lass a-sitting on your knee;
With a pint of good strong porter she makes a lovely ring,
She'll make your farmer happier than a prince or a king.

Danny Boy

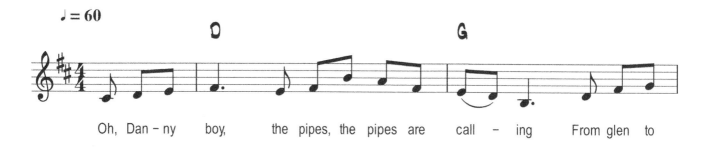

Oh, Dan – ny boy, the pipes, the pipes are call – ing From glen to

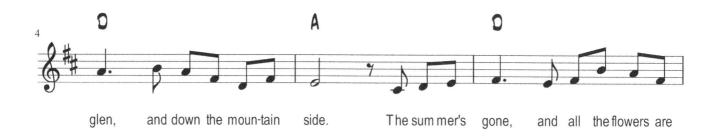

glen, and down the moun-tain side. The sum mer's gone, and all the flowers are

dy – ing 'Tis you, 'tis you must go and I must bide. But come you

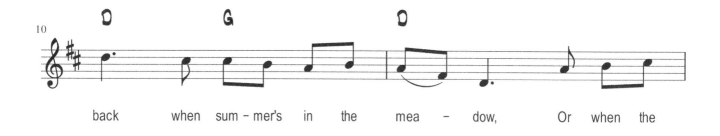

back when sum-mer's in the mea – dow, Or when the

val – ley's hushed and white with snow. 'Tis I'll be there in sun shine or in

Arrangements © 2016 www.tradschool.com

sha - dow   Oh, Dan – ny   boy, oh, Dan – ny   boy,   I   love you   so.

Oh Danny boy, the pipes, the pipes are calling
From glen to glen, and down the mountain side
The summer's gone, and all the flowers are dying
'Tis you, 'tis you must go and I must bide.

But come ye back when summer's in the meadow
Or when the valley's hushed and white with snow
'Tis I'll be here in sunshine or in shadow
Oh Danny boy, oh Danny boy, I love you so.

But when he come, and all the flowers are dying
If I am dead, as dead I well may be
You'll come and find the place where I am lying
And kneel and say an "Ave" there for me.

And I shall hear, tho' soft you tread above me
And all my grave will warm and sweeter be
For you will bend and tell me that you love me
And I shall sleep in peace until you come to me.

Arrangements © 2016 www.tradschool.com

Do You Love An Apple?

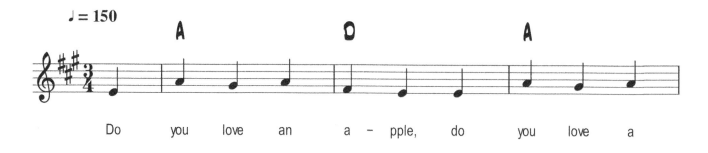

Do you love an a – pple, do you love a

pear? Do you love a la – ddie with

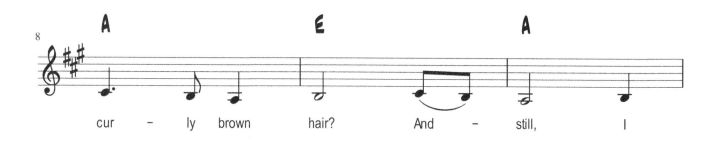

cur – ly brown hair? And – still, I

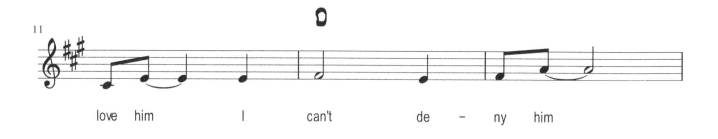

love him I can't de – ny him

I will go with him where – e – ver he goes

Arrangements © 2016 www.tradschool.com

Do you love an apple, do you love a pear?
Do you love a laddie with curly brown hair?

Chorus:
And still, I love him, I can't deny him
I'll be with him where ever he goes

Before I got married I wore a black shawl
But now that I'm married I wear bugger-all

(Chorus)

He stood at the corner, a fag in his mouth
Two hands in his pockets, he whistled me out

(Chorus)

He works at the pier, for nine pound a week,
Saturday night he comes rolling home drunk

(Chorus)

Before I got married I'd sport and I'd play
But now, the cradle gets in me way

(Chorus)

Do you love an apple, do you love a pear?
Do you love a laddie with curly brown hair?
And still, I love him, I can't deny him
I'll be with him where ever he goes

The Leaving of Liverpool

♩ = 100

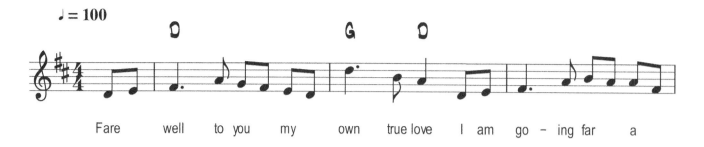

Fare well to you my own true love I am go – ing far a

way I am bound for Ca li for – ni – a But I

know that I'll re – turn some day So fare thee well, my

own true love And when I re – turn, u – ni – ted we will be It's not the

lea – ving of Li – ver – pool that grieves – me But, my

Arrangements © 2016 www.tradschool.com

dar - ling, when I think of thee

Farewell to you my own true love
I am going far away
I am bound for California
But I know that I'll return some day

Chorus:
So fare thee well, my own true love
And when I return, united we will be
It's not the leaving of Liverpool that grieves me
But, my darling, when I think of thee

I have sailed on a yankee sailing ship
Davy Crockett is her name
And Burgess is the captain of her
And they say she is a floating shame

(Chorus)

I have sailed with Burgess once before
And I think I know him right well
If a man is a sailor, he can get along
But if not than he's surely in hell

(Chorus)

Oh, the fog is on the harbour love
And I wish I could remain
But I know it will be some long time
Before I see you again

(Chorus)

The Black Velvet Band

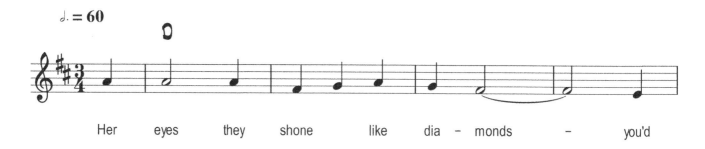

Her eyes they shone like dia – monds – you'd

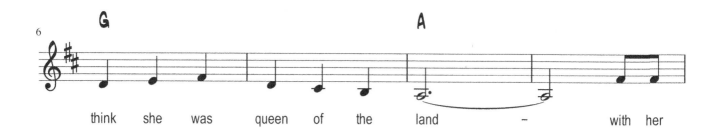

think she was queen of the land – with her

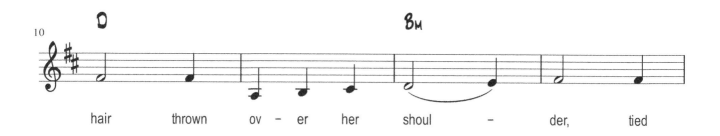

hair thrown ov – er her shoul – der, tied

up in a black vel – vet band

Arrangements © 2016 www.tradschool.com

Well, in a neat little town they call Belfast, apprentice to trade I was bound
Many an hours sweet happiness, have I spent in that neat little town
A sad misfortune came over me, which caused me to stray from the land
Far away from my friends and relations, betrayed by the black velvet band

Chorus:
Her eyes they shone like diamonds
I thought her the queen of the land
And her hair it hung over her shoulder
Tied up with a black velvet band

(Chorus)

I took a stroll down Broadway, meaning not long for to stay
When who should I meet but this pretty fair maid a' tripping along the highway
She was both fair and handsome, her neck it was just like a swans
And her hair it hung over her shoulder, tied up with a black velvet band

(Chorus)

I took a stroll with this pretty fair maid, and a gentleman passing us by
Well I knew she meant the doing of him, by the look in her roguish black eye
A goldwatch she took from his pocket and placed it right in to my hand
And the very first thing that I said was bad luck to the black velvet band

(Chorus)

Before the judge and the jury, next morning I had to appear
The judge he says to me: "Young man, your case it is proven clear
We'll give you seven years penal servitude, to be spent faraway from the land
Far away from your friends and companions, betrayed by the black velvet band"

(Chorus)

So come all you jolly young fellows a warning take by me
When you are out on the town me lads, beware of them pretty colleens
For they feed you with strong drink, until you are unable to stand
And the very next thing that you'll know is you've landed in Van Diemens Land

(Chorus)

My Own Dear Galway Bay

'Tis far a – way I am to – day from scenes I

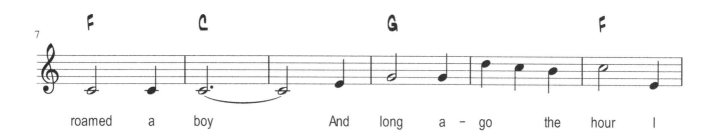

roamed a boy And long a – go the hour I

know I first saw I – lli – nois But time nor

tide nor wa – ters wide can wean my hea – rt a –

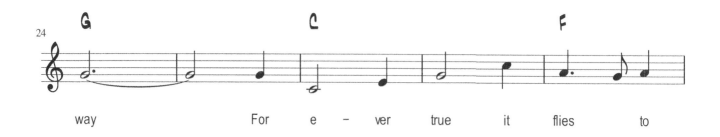

way For e – ver true it flies to

Arrangements © 2016 www.tradschool.com

you,   my   dear   old   Gal –   way   Bay.

'Tis far away I am today from scenes I roamed a boy,
And long ago the hour I know I first saw Illinois;
But time nor tide nor waters wide can wean my heart away,
For ever true it flies to you, my dear old Galway Bay.

My chosen bride is by my side, her brown hair silver-grey,
Her daughter Rose as like her grows as April dawn to day.
Our only boy, his mother's joy, his father's pride and stay;
With gifts like these I'd live at ease, were I near Galway Bay.

Oh, grey and bleak, by shore and creek, the rugged rocks abound,
But sweet and green the grass between, as grows on Irish ground,
So friendship fond, all wealth beyond, and love that lives alway,
Bless each poor home beside your foam, my dear old Galway Bay.

A prouder man I'd walk the land in health and peace of mind,
If I might toil and strive and moil, nor cast one thought behind,
But what would be the world to me, its wealth and rich array,
If memory I lost of thee, my own dear Galway Bay.

Had I youth's blood and hopeful mood and heart of fire once more,
For all the gold the world might hold I'd never quit your shore,
I'd live content whate'er God sent with neighbours old and gray,
And lay my bones, 'neath churchyard stones, beside you, Galway Bay.

The blessing of a poor old man be with you night and day,
The blessing of a lonely man whose heart will soon be clay;
'Tis all the Heaven I'll ask of God upon my dying day,
My soul to soar for evermore above you, Galway Bay.

The Bantry Girls' Lament

Oh Who will plough the fi – elds now and who will sow – the corn? And –

Who will mind the sheep now and keep them neat – ly shorn? The

stack that's in the ha – ggard un – thrashed it may – re – main Since –

John – ny went a-thrash – ing the cru – el king of Spain

Arrangements © 2016 www.tradschool.com

Oh, who will plough the fields now and who will sow the corn?
Who will mind the sheep now and keep them neatly shorn?
The stack that's in the haggard, unthrashed it may remain
Since Johnny's went a-thrashing the cruel king of Spain

The girls from the bawnogue in sorrow may retire
And the piper and his bellows go home and blow the fire
Since Johnny, lovely Johnny is sailing o'er the main
Along with other patriots to fight the King of Spain

The boys will surely miss him when Moneymore comes round
And they'll find that their bold captain is nowhere to be found
And the peelers must stand idle, all against their will and main
Since the gallant boys who gave them work now peels the King of Spain

At wakes or hurling matches your like we'll never see
Till you come back to us again a stor gra geal mo chroi
And won't you thrash the buckeens that show us much disdain
Because our eyes are not so bright as those you'll meet in Spain

If cruel fate will not permit our Johnny to return
His heavy loss we Bantry girls will never cease to mourn
We'll resign ourselves to our sad lot and die in grief and pain
Since Johnny died for Ireland's pride in the foreign land of Spain

High Germany

♩ = 90

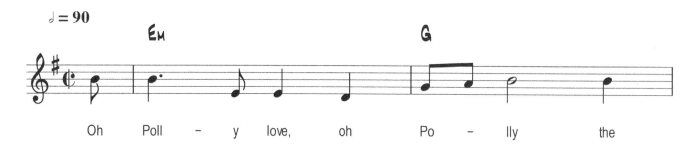

Oh Poll – y love, oh Po – lly the

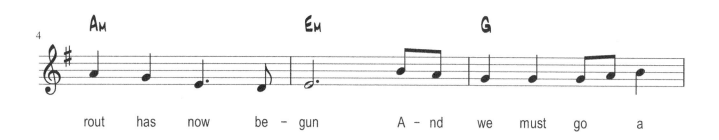

rout has now be – gun   A – nd we must go a

mar – ching at the beat – ing of the drum   Go

dress your – se – lf a – ll in your best and come a – long with

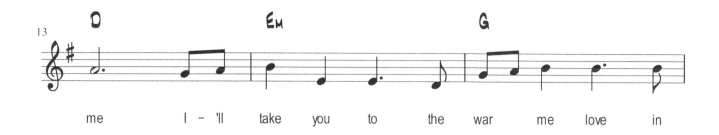

me   I – 'll take you to the war me love in

Arrangements © 2016 www.tradschool.com

High   Ger – ma – ny

Oh Polly love, oh Polly the rout has now begun
And we must go a marching at the beating of the drum
Go dress yourself all in your best and come along with me
I'll take you to the war me love in High Germany

Oh Willy love, oh Willy come list to what I say
My feet they are so tender, I can not march away
And besides my dearest Willy I am with child by thee
Not fitted for the war me love in High Germany

I'll buy for you a horse me love and on it you shall ride
And all my life I'll be there riding by your side
We'll stop at every ale-house and drink when we are dry
We'll be true to one another, get married bye and bye

Oh cursed be the cruel wars that ever they should rise
And out of merry England press many a man likewise
They pressed my true love from me, likewise my brothers three
And sent them to the wars me lad in High Germany

My friends I do not value nor my foes I do not fear
Now my love has left me I wander far and near
And when my baby it is born and smiling on my knee
I'll think of lovely Willy in High Germany

Oh Polly love, oh Polly the rout has now begun
And we must go a marching at the beating of the drum
Go dress yourself all in your best and come along with me
I'll take you to the war me love in High Germany

Arrangements © 2016 www.tradschool.com

Johnny I Hardly Knew Ye

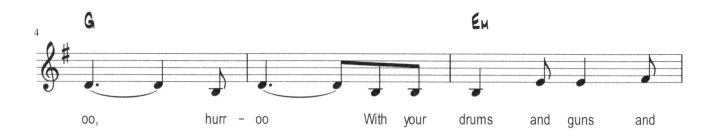

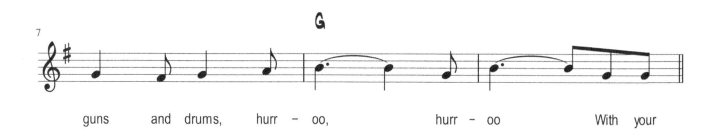

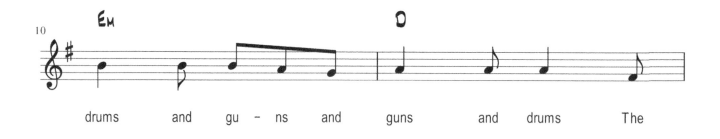

look   so   queer   Joh – nny   I   har – dly   knew   ye

While goin' the road to sweet Athy, hurroo, hurroo
While goin' the road to sweet Athy, hurroo, hurroo
While goin' the road to sweet Athy
A stick in me hand and a tear in me eye
A doleful damsel I heard cry,
Johnny I hardly knew ye.

Chorus:
With your drums and guns and guns and drums,
hurroo, hurroo
With your drums and guns and guns and drums,
hurroo, hurroo
With your drums and guns and guns and drums
The enemy nearly slew ye
Oh my darling dear, Ye look so queer
Johnny I hardly knew ye.

Where are the eyes that looked so mild,
hurroo, hurroo
Where are the eyes that looked so mild,
hurroo, hurroo
Where are the eyes that looked so mild
When my poor heart you first beguiled
Why did ye scadaddle from me and the child
Oh Johnny, I hardly knew ye.

(Chorus)

Where are your legs that used to run,
hurroo, hurroo
Where are your legs that used to run,
hurroo, hurroo
Where are your legs that used to run
When you went to carry a gun
Indeed your dancing days are done
Oh Johnny, I hardly knew ye.

(Chorus)

I'm happy for to see ye home, hurroo, hurroo
I'm happy for to see ye home, hurroo, hurroo
I'm happy for to see ye home
All from the island of Ceylon
So low in the flesh, so high in the bone
Oh Johnny I hardly knew ye.

(Chorus)

Ye haven't an arm, ye haven't a leg,
hurroo, hurroo
Ye haven't an arm, ye haven't a leg,
hurroo, hurroo
Ye haven't an arm, ye haven't a leg
Ye're an armless, boneless, chickenless egg
Ye'll have to be put with a bowl out to beg
Oh Johnny I hardly knew ye.

(Chorus)

They're rolling out the guns again,
hurroo, hurroo
They're rolling out the guns again,
hurroo, hurroo
They're rolling out the guns again
But they never will take my sons again
No they'll never take my sons again
Johnny I'm swearing to ye.

I'll Tell My Ma

Arrangements © 2016 www.tradschool.com

I'll tell my ma, when I get home
The boys won't leave the girls alone
They pull my hair, they stole my comb
But that's alright, till I go home
She is handsome, she is pretty
She is the belle of Belfast city
She is a-courting one, two, three
Pray, can you tell me who is she?

Albert Mooney says he loves her
All the boys are fightin' for her
Knock at the door, they're ringing the bell
"Hello, my true love are you well?"
Out she comes white as snow
Rings on her fingers, bells on her toes
Ol' Jenny Murray says she'll die
If she doesn't get the fellow with the roving eye

Let the wind and the rain and the hail blow high
And the snow come traveling through the sky
She's as sweet as apple pie
She'll get her own right by and by
When she gets a lad of her own
She won't tell her ma when she gets home
Let them all come as they will
It's Albert Mooney she loves still

I'll tell my ma, when I get home
The boys won't leave the girls alone
They pull my hair, they stole my comb
But that's alright till I get home
She is handsome, she is pretty
She is the belle Belfast city
She is a-courting one, two, three
Pray, can you tell me who is she?

Lanigan's Ball

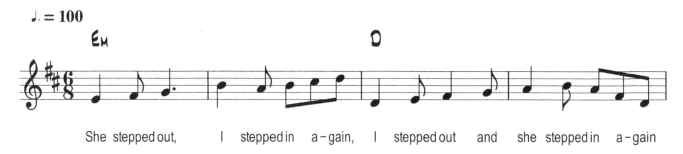

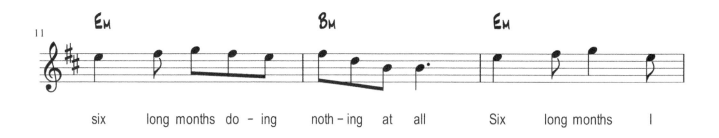

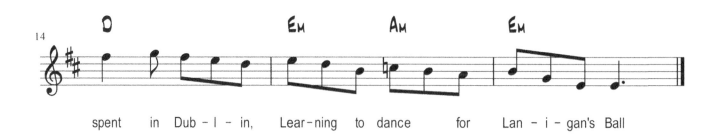

Arrangements © 2016 www.tradschool.com

In the town of Athy one Jeremy Lannigan, battered away 'til he hadn't a pound
His father he died and made him a man again, left him a farm and ten acres of ground
He gave a grand party to friends and relations who didn't forget him when come to the wall
And if you but listen I'll make your eyes glisten at rows and ructions at Lannigan's Ball

Myself to be sure, got free invitations for all the nice boys and girls that I ask
In less than a minute the friends and relations were dancing as merry as bees round a cask
There were lashing of punch and wine for the ladies potatoes and cake, bacon and tea
There were the Nolan, Dolans, O'Grady's courting the girls and dancing away

They were doing all kinds of nonsensical polkas all around in a whirligig
Julia and I soon banished their nonsense out on the floor for a reel and jig
How the girls all got mad at me danced till they thought the ceilings would fall
I spent six months in Brooks Academy learning to dance for Lannigan's Ball

Chorus:
Six long months I spent in Dublin, six long months doing nothing at all
Six long months I spent in Dublin learning to dance for Lannigan's Ball
She stepped out, I stepped in again, I stepped out and she stepped in again
She stepped out, I stepped in again to dance for Lannigan's Ball

The boys were merry the girls all hearty dancing around in couples and groups
An accident happened; Terence McCarthy put his right boot through Miss Finnerty's hoops
The creature she fainted and cried bloody murder, called for her brothers and gathered they all
Carmody swore he'd go no further yill he got revenge at Lannigan's Ball

(Chorus)

Boys oh boys 'tis then there was ructions I got a kick from young Phelim McHugh
I soon replied to his fine introduction kicked him a terrible hullabaloo
Casey the piper was near gettin' strangled they leapt on his pipes, bellows, chanter and all
Boys and girls all got entangled and that put an end to Lannigan's Ball

(Chorus)

The Rising of the Moon

By the ri – sing of the moon–, by the ri – sing of the moon   The

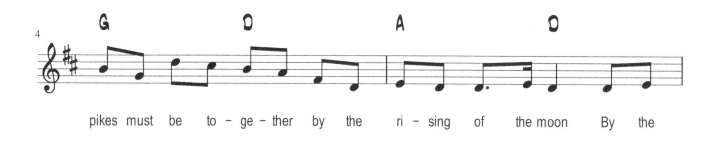

pikes must be to – ge – ther by the ri – sing of the moon   By the

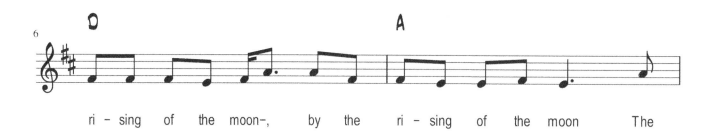

ri – sing of the moon–, by the ri – sing of the moon   The

pikes must be to – ge – ther by the ri – sing of the moon

Arrangements © 2016 www.tradschool.com

And come tell me Sean O'Farrell tell me why you hurry so
Hush, a buachaill! hush and listen and his cheeks were all aglow
I bear orders from the captain, get you ready quick and soon
For the pikes must be together by the rising of the moon

Chorus:
By the rising of the moon, by the rising of the moon
For the pikes must be together by the rising of the moon

And come tell me Sean O'Farrell where the gathering is to be
At the old spot by the river quite well known to you and me
One more word for signal token whistle out the marching tune
With your pike upon your shoulder by the rising of the moon

(Chorus)

Out from many a mud wall cabin eyes were watching through the night
Many a manly heart was beating for the blessed warning light
Murmurs rang along the valleys to the banshees lonely croon
And a thousand pikes were flashing by the rising of the moon

(Chorus)

All along that singing river that black mass of men was seen
High above their shining weapons flew their own beloved green
Death to every foe and traitor! Whistle out the marching tune
And hurrah, me boys, for freedom, 'tis the rising of the moon

(Chorus)

'Tis the rising of the moon, 'tis the rising of the moon
And hurrah, me boys, for freedom, 'tis the rising of the moon

The Good Ship Kangaroo

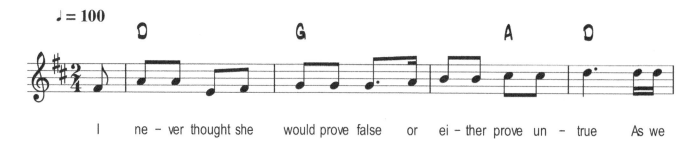

Once I was a waiting man who lived at home at ease
Now I am a mariner that ploughs the stormy seas
I always loved seafaring life I bid my love adieu
I shipped as steward and cook me boys on board the kangaroo

Chorus:
I never thought she would prove false or either prove untrue
As we sailed away from Milford Bay on board the Kangaroo

Think of me oh think of me she mournfully did say
When you are in a foreign land and I am far away
And take this lucky thrupenny bit it will make you bear in mind
This loving trusting faithful heart you left in tears behind (Chorus)

Cheer up, cheer up my own true love don't weep so bitterly
She sobbed she sighed she choked she cried till she could not say goodbye
I won't be gone for very long but for a month or two
And when I return again of course I'll visit you (Chorus)

Our ship it was homeward bound from manys the foreign shore
Manys the foreign present unto my love I bore
I brought tortoises from Tenerife and ties from Timbuktu
A China rat, a Bengal cat and a Bombay cockatoo (Chorus)

Paid off I sought her dwelling on a street above the town
Where an ancient dame upon the line was hanging out her gown
Where is my love? she's vanished sir about six months ago
With a smart young man who drives the van for Chaplin Son (Chorus)

ALSO AVAILABLE

Irish Music - 400 Traditional Tunes

184 pages, with audio download

Classic Irish Session Tunes from the author of "A Complete Guide to Playing Irish Traditional Music on the Whistle". A unique collection of the most popular tunes played in Ireland … and throughout the world. Complete with 400-track audio download of each tune played at moderate speed on Tin Whistle.

Stephen Ducke is an Irish flute and whistle player from County Roscommon. Musician for over 30 years and an inspired teacher, he has recorded one solo album and is author and editor of several books of Irish and traditional music.

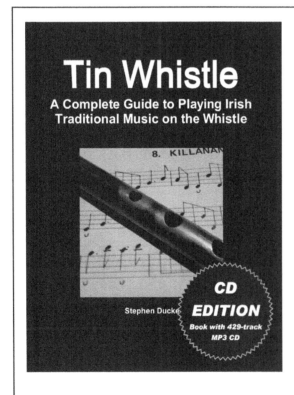

A Complete Guide to Playing Irish Traditional Music on the Whistle

286 pages; with 429 accompanying audio tracks

This tutor book, with its accompanying audio files, is intended to give a complete introduction to playing Irish music in the traditional style on the tin whistle; it covers all from the very first notes on the instruments to the most advances ornamentation. The book is broadly divided into two parts, with the shorter first part covering the basics of the whistle (pages 1-48) while the longer second part (pages 49-286) covers the playing of Irish traditional music on the instrument.

It is intended for anybody who wants to play traditional music in the Irish style, from complete beginners to confirmed or advanced players who wish to work on their style or ornamentation. Tablature as well as sheet music is used throughout the book, so it is accessible to the complete beginner; while more advanced players will appreciate the attention to detail in style and ornamentation in the later parts of the book.

THE TUNEBOOK SERIES

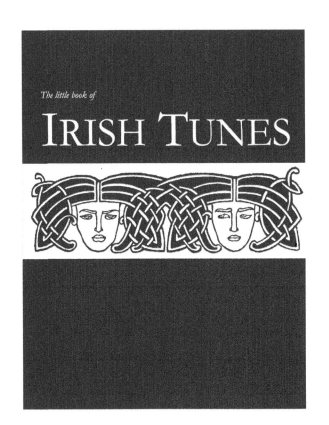

The little book of

IRISH TUNES

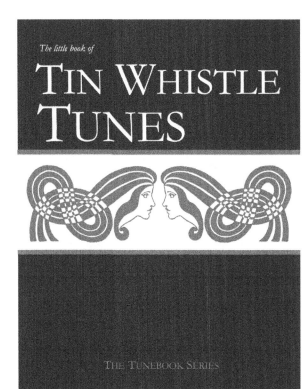

The little book of

TIN WHISTLE TUNES

THE TUNEBOOK SERIES

The little book of

CELTIC MUSIC

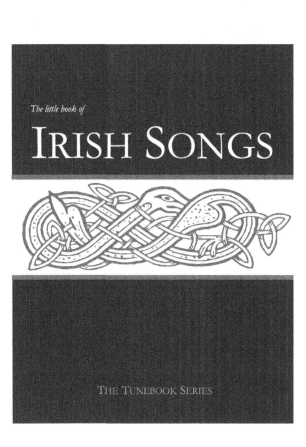

The little book of

IRISH SONGS

THE TUNEBOOK SERIES

TIN WHISTLE FOR BEGINNERS

Tin Whistle for Beginners : easy Irish songs and Tunes with fingering guides for Tin Whistle

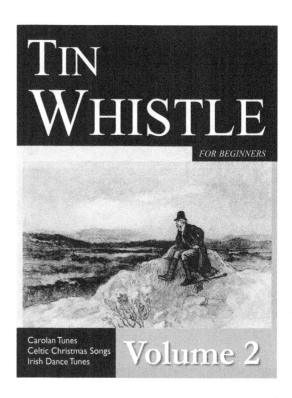

Whistle for Kids : easy tin whistle tunes for children

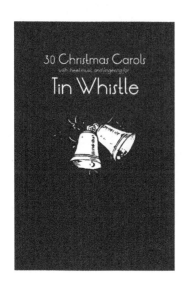

Made in United States
North Haven, CT
05 April 2025

67608040R00030